# JUST LIKE US! PLANTS

For Brendan Heos —B.H.

The illustrations in this book were done in pen and ink, watercolor, and digital media.

The text type was set in Agenda and Felt-Tip Woman.
The display type was hand-lettered by David Clark.

*Library of Congress Cataloging-in-Publication Data*
Names: Heos, Bridget, author. | Clark, David, 1960 March 19– illustrator.
Title: Just like us!, plants / by Bridget Heos ; illustrations by David Clark.
Other titles: Plants
Description: Boston ; New York : Houghton Mifflin Harcourt, [2018] |
Audience: Ages 4–8. | Audience: K to grade 3.
Identifiers: LCCN 2016037281 | ISBN 9780544570948 (hardcover)
Subjects: LCSH: Plants—Juvenile literature. | Plants—Adaptation—Juvenile literature.
Classification: LCC QK912 .H46 2018 | DDC 580—dc23
LC record available at https://lccn.loc.gov/2016037281

Manufactured in China
SCP 10 9 8 7 6 5 4 3 2 1
4500709332

| Lexile Level | Guided Reading | Fountas & Pinnell | Interest Level |
| --- | --- | --- | --- |
| 850 | P | P | Grades K–3 |

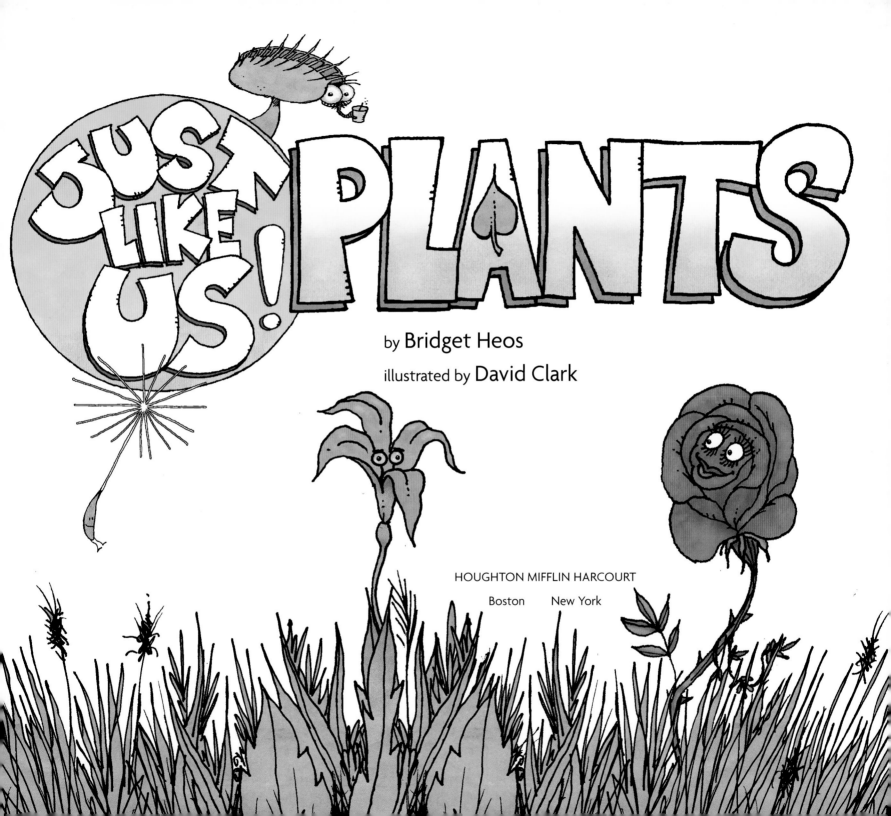

# JUST LIKE US! PLANTS

by Bridget Heos

illustrated by David Clark

HOUGHTON MIFFLIN HARCOURT

Boston     New York

# PLANTS

## The Inside Scoop

**PEOPLE THINK,** talk, and walk around. Plants do none of these things. So how can they be anything like us? Well, did you know that plant leaves communicate with one another? Plants also wear perfume . . . and cunning disguises. They even wage war, using battle armor and weapons. Read on to learn all about our bodacious botanical friends—and how they're just like us.

# SUNLIGHT: IT'S WHAT'S FOR DINNER.

**WHETHER AT THE BEACH,** ball game, or park, people love to bask in the sun. Plants do too. But they don't just soak up the rays. To them, it's dinner. Leaves—whether flat like an oak leaf or skinny like a pine needle—absorb sunlight. Then, in a process known as photosynthesis, they turn sunlight, water, nutrients, and carbon dioxide into plant food.

Just as people reach for a snack when they're hungry, leaves grow toward open sunlight. Eventually, every patch of light is filled—which is why trees provide such perfect shade. Meanwhile, plants in the shade grow larger leaves in order to absorb as much sunlight as possible. The leaves of some aroid plants, for instance, grow to ten feet long and three feet across. Unbe-leaf-able!

**Just breathe.** People breathe in oxygen and exhale carbon dioxide. Plants do the opposite: they absorb carbon dioxide through pores in their leaves, and then release oxygen through the same pores. The carbon then becomes part of the plant. A forty-year-old tree can store one ton of carbon—the weight of a rhinoceros! In this way, plants help to slow climate change, which is caused by carbon dioxide and other greenhouse gases.

# BE SURE TO DRINK EIGHT THOUSAND GLASSES OF WATER A DAY

**PEOPLE NEED WATER** to be healthy. But we lose water through breathing, sweating, and going to the bathroom. That's why many people try to drink eight glasses of water a day. Trees lose water too. In a process called transpiration, water evaporates from pores in the tree's leaves. It's the tree equivalent of sweating!

An NBA player produces more sweat than a kid shooting hoops, and the bigger the tree, the more it "sweats" too. One of the tallest trees on Earth, the *Eucalyptus regnans*, loses hundreds of gallons per day through transpiration. So it must soak up thousands of glasses of water daily. The water comes up through the roots and follows a system of long, hollow, connected cells until it reaches the topmost leaves, which can be as high as 325 feet. That's a tall drink of water!

**Oh, were you going to drink that?** The Australian Christmas tree blooms during the hot, dry summer (Christmastime in Australia). To get the water its flowers need, the tree does something rather Grinch-y. Its roots encircle and slice through the roots of neighboring plants. Then the Christmas tree sucks up all their water for itself. Happy holidays . . . gulp!

# COME FOR THE NECTAR; STAY TO GET EATEN ALIVE.

**MOST PLANTS GET THEIR NUTRITION** from water (which has absorbed nutrients from the soil). But in some environments, the soil has hardly any nutrition at all. So plants have adapted to eating meat in the form of flies. The Venus flytrap grows in the marshes of North and South Carolina. Each leaf has two spiky lobes that release nectar—the Kool-Aid of the insect world. Smelling the delicious juice, the fly lands on the leaf. But when it touches the spikes, the lobes snap shut. As the fly struggles, the plant releases hydrochloric acid—stomach acid—and digests the insect alive. Mmm . . . nothing like a side of flies!

# SAY IT WITH *Flowers*

**WITH THE RIGHT MIX OF SUNLIGHT,** water, and nutrition, plants grow up and have babies—just like people. A plant baby is a seed! Before the seed can grow, pollen from the plant's stamen (the male part of the flower) must fertilize the plant's eggs in the pistil (the female part of the flower). Sometimes, this happens within a single plant. Other times, the pollen and eggs come from two different plants. In that case, plants rely on animals to transport the pollen.

Plants attract animals with a dab of perfume. Like the aroma of chocolate chip cookies wafting from the kitchen, a flower's smell tells animals there's a sugary treat inside—nectar. Insects, birds, and small mammals flock to the flowers. As they sip the delicious nectar and eat the nutritious pollen, some of the pollen sticks to the animals. When they visit the next flower, they bring the pollen with them and deposit it onto that flower's eggs. A seed is born. Thanks, animal friends!

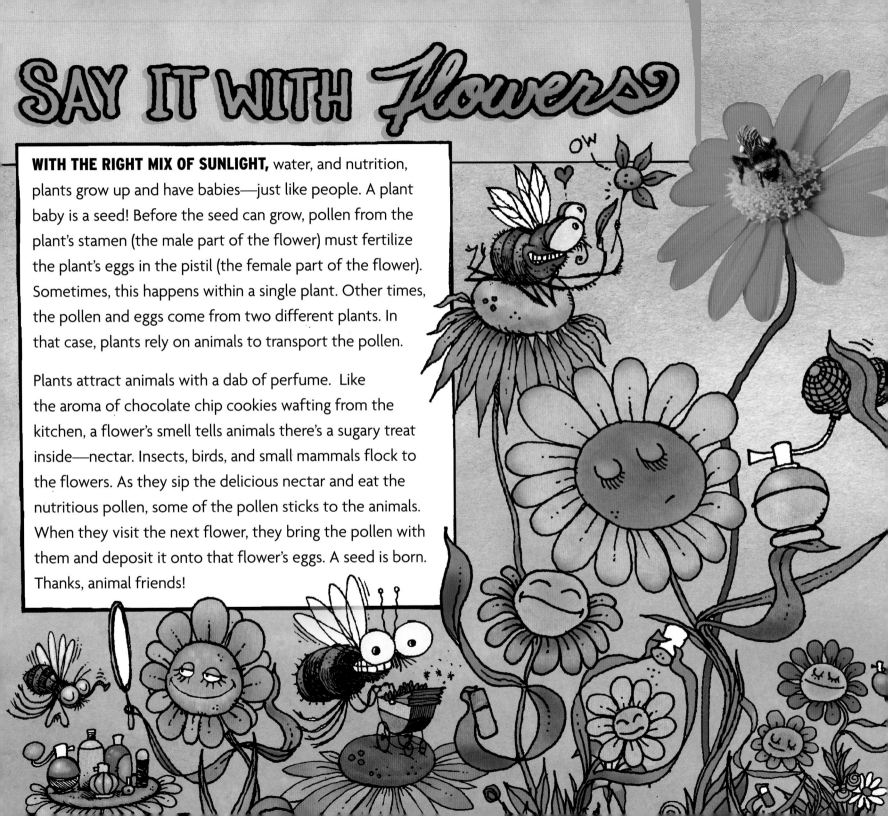

# Eau de DEAD HORSE

**PURPLISH PINK, THICK, AND FLESHY**, the dead horse arum lily looks—and smells—like rotting flesh. Blowflies can't resist! They swarm the lily and burrow deep inside, where it is extra warm and stinky—just like the inside of a dead horse. Yum! There, they drink the nectar and pollinate the flower. Sadly, so many flies visit the putrid lily that the exit is often blocked and the flies die inside. In the end, the delicious dead horse smell was simply too good—I mean, bad—to be true.

# BEE MINE

**FLOWERS DON'T ATTRACT ANIMALS** just by wearing perfume, but by "dressing up" too. People wear costumes on Halloween. The mirror orchid wears a disguise all the time. It looks like a flower with a female bee resting on the top. It even smells like a female bee. A male makes a bee line for the flower, hoping to mate with the female. When he lands, a petal from the orchid folds over and places pollen on his head. Undeterred, he visits the next "bee." A petal on the new flower folds over, but this time, the bee deposits the pollen onto the petal. He visits several more flowers before realizing they are not really bees. What a buzzkill!

**Picking flowers:** Different flowers attract different animals. For instance, pale flowers can be seen at night, so they attract nocturnal creatures such as bats and moths. Colorful flowers attract butterflies and birds, which fly by day. Butterflies alight on fragrant flowers. But the flowers birds pollinate—such as poinsettias—don't have strong scents. That's because many pollinating birds lack a good sense of smell. They're smeller blind!

# APPLES to APPLES

**ONCE POLLINATED, A PLANT PRODUCES SEEDS.** Lots of them, actually. An apple tree, for instance, can produce four hundred apples in a season, each containing several seeds. They say the apple doesn't fall far from the tree, but in order to get sunlight, seeds must leave their parent's shady side. Unlike humans, they can't walk away. But they have their own ways of getting around.

Some catch a ride inside an animal's belly. Like flowers, fruit is colorful and sweet-smelling so that it will attract the attention of animals. They eat the fruit, digesting all but the seeds. The seeds wind up in the animals' poop, and this provides fertilizer to help the seeds grow. Not all seeds become plants, of course. Some never get the proper water and sunlight. And that's a good thing. What if every apple tree produced more than four hundred new apple trees each spring? Apples would soon take over the world!

**Stinky-cheese fruit:** Sometimes a fruit's yumminess is in the eye—or rather the nose—of the beholder. Durian fruit grows in Malaysia and Indonesia. Its smell has been compared to that of pig poop, rotten onions, and dead people. The fruit is so smelly that it is banned on Singapore subways. And yet animals and people alike are drawn to it. They hack through its prickly skin and suck the white, creamy fruit surrounding the seeds, which is reportedly delicious in that stinky-cheese way.

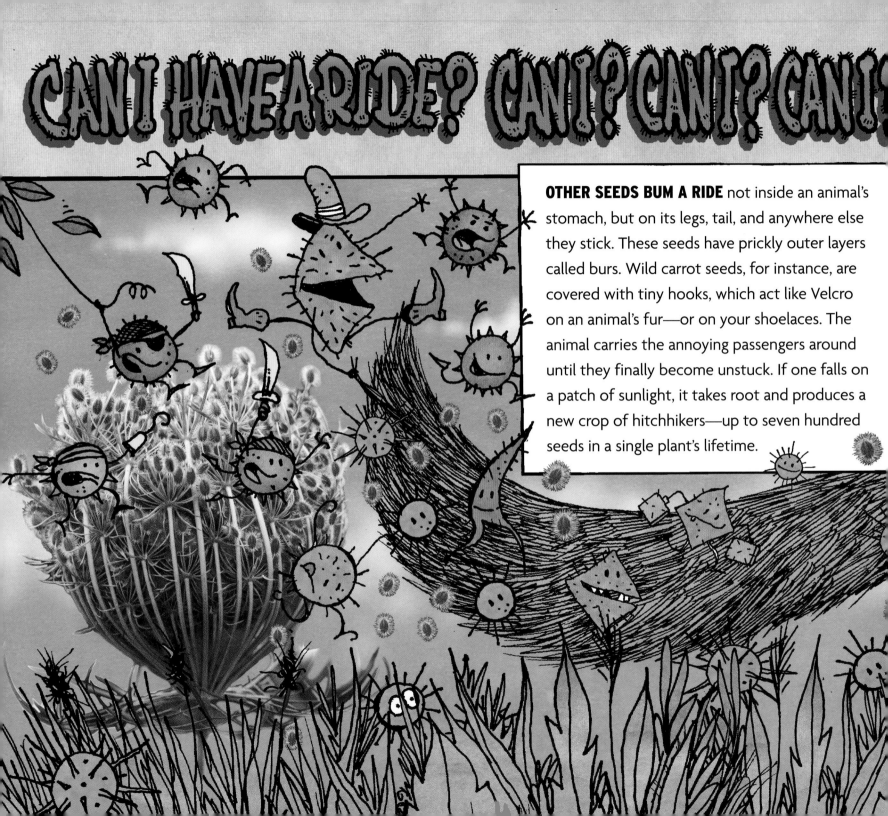

**OTHER SEEDS BUM A RIDE** not inside an animal's stomach, but on its legs, tail, and anywhere else they stick. These seeds have prickly outer layers called burs. Wild carrot seeds, for instance, are covered with tiny hooks, which act like Velcro on an animal's fur—or on your shoelaces. The animal carries the annoying passengers around until they finally become unstuck. If one falls on a patch of sunlight, it takes root and produces a new crop of hitchhikers—up to seven hundred seeds in a single plant's lifetime.

# COCONUT CRUISE

**COCONUTS ARE FRUITS TOO.** But they *don't* bum rides. They're the luxury travelers of the plant world. A cruise? Don't mind if I do! Coconut trees grow on beaches—just above the high tide line. When ripe, the fruits fall from the tree and make their way down the slope of the beach, where the tide washes them out to sea. Bon voyage!

Coconuts are perfectly designed for the ocean journey. Their hairy outsides are strong and waterproof. Their insides are partially hollow—making them light enough to float. Finally, they take a long time to sprout—up to 220 days—which is important because if they sprout while in the ocean, they'll die. When the coconut arrives safely on the next shore, the new roots soak up the coconut juice and absorb nutrients from the coconut meat. Finally, the tree takes root in the sand. Ah, another day in paradise.

# ONE OF THEM FANCY HELICOPTERS

**WHILE SOME SEEDS SET SAIL,** others fly the friendly skies. Each maple tree seed has a wing so that when it falls, it spins like a helicopter. In this way, the seed can fly far away from its parent tree. Dandelion seeds also fly, or rather float. The seeds are topped with white threads, which act as parachutes and can carry the seeds for miles on a windy day.

# THAT'S NOT A THORN. THIS IS A THORN!

**PLANTS DON'T MIND WHEN** animals mooch some nectar, pollen, or fruit. But if a hungry critter takes a bite out of a leaf, that means war! After all, plants need their leaves for soaking up sunlight. Plants use a variety of weapons to defend themselves. Like people, they wear armor—in the form of spines, thorns, and prickles.

Spines, such as those on a cactus, grow like leaves. Thorns grow in the same way as branches, and tend to be long and strong. Prickles grow on the surface of a plant—and are more easily broken off than thorns. Contrary to poetry, every rose does not have a thorn. Every rose has a prickle. Luckily for the rose, a thorn by any other name still hurts, and most animals don't like eating sharp objects of any kind—whether a thorn, spine, or prickle.

# LEAF ME ALONE!

**DURING AN INVASION,** people fight back. Plants do too, and their weapons are quite painful. Stinging nettle, for instance, has tiny hairs on its stems and leaves. If you touch the plant, the hairs break off, cutting your skin and releasing chemicals that burn and sting. People touch stinging nettle only accidentally. Rabbits and other animals avoid eating the plant altogether. Caterpillars, on the other hand, munch away, somehow avoiding the painful stings.

# CATERPILLAR BIT ME, AND IT REALLY HURT!

**SOME LEAVES WORK TOGETHER** to unleash their poison on hungry caterpillars. When leaves from a tomato plant are eaten by caterpillars, those leaves sound the alarm. The other leaves receive the message and produce poison. This poison makes the insects unable to digest the tomato leaves. Good teamwork, tomatoes!

**Actually, two heads are NOT better than one.**

African bugleweed has the most grotesque weaponry of all. The plant produces a chemical similar to caterpillar growth hormones, but it causes abnormal growth. At first, nothing happens to the caterpillar after eating the plant. But when it metamorphoses into a butterfly, it grows two heads and dies. Needless to say, butterflies avoid laying eggs on this plant. At least, those that have one good head on their shoulders do.

# THE TAKING TREE

**PLANTS AREN'T ALWAYS** on the defensive. They wage war on other plants too. Vines are the pirates of the plant world—stealing sunlight by climbing up their host trees. Some vines are harmless. Others, like the strangler fig tree, are killers. When fig vine seeds land on the branches of another tree, they sprout. Their roots grow over the tree until they reach the ground. Soaking up water and nutrients from the soil, the roots strengthen and grow. Soon, the roots cover the tree so that the trunk can no longer expand. At the same time, the fig leaves tower over the host's leaves, robbing them of sunlight. The tree dies and rots away. By now the vines can stand on their own, so the strangler fig . . . well, it just doesn't give a fig.

# An Eggcellent Disguise

**PLANTS USE DISGUISE NOT JUST** to attract pollinators but for defense, too. *Heliconius* butterflies lay their eggs on the passion vine, which is what their caterpillars eat. But if mama insect sees other eggs on the plant, she flies off to a different vine. After all, caterpillars eat a lot and she wants to make sure her babies will only have to share with each other. To fool the butterfly, the plant produces yellow bumps that look like eggs. This tells the butterfly, "Move along, there is nothing to eat here."

Experts at disguise, heroes on the battlefield, and sweet-smelling to boot, plants really are a lot like us. Not to get too flowery, but perhaps next time you stop to smell the roses, you should tip your hat to them too.

# SAY WHAT?

**bur** the prickly outer layer of some seeds.

**carbon dioxide** a gas in the Earth's atmosphere that is absorbed by plants.

**fertilizer** a substance that helps plants to grow.

**growth hormone** a substance produced by a living thing in order to stimulate growth.

**hydrochloric acid** a gas produced by Venus flytraps to digest flies; it is also produced in the human stomach to help digest food.

**nectar** a sweet liquid secreted by plants.

**nocturnal** most active at night.

**nutrients** substances that help a living thing grow.

**oxygen** a gas in the Earth's atmosphere that plants release during the process of photosynthesis.

**photosynthesis** the process by which plants turn sunlight, water, nutrients, and carbon dioxide into food.

**pistil** the female part of a flower.

**pollen** microscopic grains (which collectively look like yellow powder) produced by the male part of the flower.

**pollinate** to apply pollen to the female part of the flower in order to produce a seed.

**pores** tiny openings on the surface of plants that allow plants to absorb carbon dioxide and release oxygen and water vapor.

**prickle** a sharp appendage jutting out from the surface of a plant.

**roots** the part of a plant that usually grows underground, soaking up water and nutrients.

**spine** a sharp leaf, as in a cactus spine, or the sharp edge of a leaf.

**stamen** the male part of a flower.

**thorn** a sharp appendage that grows like a branch.

**transpiration** the process by which plants absorb water and release water vapor through their pores.

# BIBLIOGRAPHY

Attenborough, David. *The Private Life of Plants*. Princeton, NJ: Princeton University Press, 1995.

BBC Two. "Death by Strangulation." *The Private Life of Plants*. November 16, 2011. (www.bbc.co.uk/programmes/p00lx5yn)

Harries, Hugh. "Germination Rate Is the Significant Characteristic Determining Coconut Palm Diversity." *Annals of Botany: Plants*. November 12, 2012. (aobpla.oxfordjournals.org/content/2012/pls045.full)

King, John. *Reaching for the Sun: How Plants Work*. Cambridge: Cambridge University Press, 1997.

North Carolina State University College of Agriculture and Life Sciences, Department of Horticultural Science, and the NC State University and NC A&T State University Cooperative Extension. "Tree Facts." (www.ncsu.edu/project/treesofstrength/treefact.htm; accessed August 19, 2016.)

Penn State Extension. "Wild Carrot." (extension.psu.edu/pests/weeds/weed-id/wild-carrot; accessed February 15, 2015.)

Ruben, Barbara. "How Dangerous Are the Thorns on a Hawthorn Tree?" SFGate.com. (homeguides.sfgate.com/dangerous-thorns-hawthorn-tree-59377.html; accessed August 19, 2016.)

Tan, Monica. "Durian: Love It or Hate It, Is This the World's Most Divisive Fruit?" *Guardian*. October 1, 2014. (www.theguardian.com/lifeandstyle/australia-food-blog/2014/oct/01/durian-the-worlds-most-divisive-fruit)

Trinklein, David. "Of Thorns, Spines, and Prickles." University of Missouri Integrated Pest Management. January 3, 2013. (ipm.missouri.edu/meg/2013/1/Of-Thorns-Spines-and-Prickles)

United States Department of Agriculture Forest Service. "Pollinator Syndromes." (www.fs.fed.us/wildflowers/pollinators/What_is_Pollination/syndromes.shtml; accessed August 19, 2016.)

USGS. "Transpiration: The Water Cycle." (water.usgs.gov/edu/watercycletranspiration.html; accessed August 19, 2016.)

**BRIDGET HEOS** is the author of more than sixty nonfiction titles for kids and teens, including *Shell, Beak, Tusk; Stronger Than Steel; It's Getting Hot in Here; I, Fly;* and *What to Expect When You're Expecting Larvae.* She's also the author of the picture books *Mustache Baby* and *Mustache Baby Meets His Match.* Bridget lives in Kansas City with her husband and four children, and you can learn more about her and her books at authorbridgetheos.com.

**DAVID CLARK** has illustrated numerous picture books including *Pirate Bob, Fractions in Disguise,* and *The Mine-o-Saur.* He also co-created—and illustrates—the nationally syndicated comic strip *Barney & Clyde.* David lives in Virginia with his family, and you can learn more about his books and his comics at sites.google.com/site/davidclark1988.